The Life and World of

BOUDICCA

Struan Reid

www.heinemann.co.uk/library
Visit our website to find out more information about Heinemann Library books.

To order:
☎ Phone 44 (0) 1865 888066
▤ Send a fax to 44 (0) 1865 314091
▯ Visit the Heinemann Library Bookshop at www.heinemann.co.uk/library to browse our catalogue and order online.

First published in Great Britain by Heinemann Library,
Halley Court, Jordan Hill, Oxford OX2 8EJ
a division of Reed Educational and Professional Publishing Ltd.
Heinemann is a registered trademark of Reed Educational & Professional Publishing Ltd.

OXFORD MELBOURNE AUCKLAND
JOHANNESBURG BLANTYRE GABORONE
IBADAN PORTSMOUTH (NH) USA CHICAGO

Designed by Celia Floyd
Illustrated by Jeff Edwards and Joanna Brooker
Originated by Ambassador Litho Ltd
Printed by Wing King Tong in Hong Kong.

ISBN 0 431 14771 X
06 05 04 03 02
10 9 8 7 6 5 4 3 2 1

British Library Cataloguing in Publication Data

Reid, Struan
   The life and world of Boudicca
   1. Boudicca, Queen, consort of Prasutagus, King of the Iceni, d. 60
   2. Queens – Great Britain – Biography – Juvenile literature
   3. Great Britain – History – Roman period, 55 B.C.–449 A.D. – Juvenile literature
   I. Title   II. Boudicca
   936.2'04'092

Acknowledgements

The Publishers would like to thank the following for permission to reproduce photographs:
Ancient Art and Architecture: pp13, 24, 27; The Art Archive: p21; British Museum: pp11, 20; Colchester Museums: p15; Colin Dixon: p9; Corbis: pp4, 25; Corbis/Annie Griffiths: p28; Corbis/Michael Nicholson: p12; Corbis/Robert Estall: p18; Corbis/© Historical Picture Archive: p14; Gloucester City Museum: p22; Museum of London: pp16, 17; National Museums and Galleries of Wales: p19; The Photolibrary Wales: p26; Werner Forman Archive: pp6, 7, 10, 23, 29.

Cover photograph reproduced with permission of Peter Evans.

Our thanks to Rebecca Vickers for her help in the preparation of this book.

Every effort has been made to contact copyright holders of any material reproduced in this book. Any omissions will be rectified in subsequent printings if notice is given to the Publisher.

Contents

Any words appearing in the text in bold, **like this**, are explained in the glossary.

Who was Boudicca?

Boudicca was a **warrior** queen who lived in Britain nearly 2000 years ago. She led her people, called the Iceni, in an **uprising** against the Roman forces who were occupying Britain at that time.

Rebellion against the Romans

With terrifying speed, Boudicca and her armies of Celtic warriors swept across south-eastern England, fighting, burning towns and killing as they went. Her **rebellion** caused terrible damage to the Roman forces and the **Celts** remained a problem for the **Roman Empire** for many years to come.

Boudicca's rebellion was like a raging fire that blew across the country, but in less than a year Boudicca was defeated by the Romans. Rather than suffer the disgrace of being dragged through the streets of Rome in a public parade, Boudicca killed herself.

A powerful female leader

Today, Boudicca is still one of the most famous characters in British history. She is remembered as a brave warrior queen who led her people in a last attempt to preserve the **independence** of the British people against the conquering armies of the Roman Empire. She was also a powerful female leader at a time when most leaders were men.

▶ This statue of Queen Boudicca driving her **chariot** stands on the banks of the River Thames in London, near the Houses of Parliament. This statue was put up in 1902.

How do we know?

We know very little about Boudicca's early life. This is because the Celts did not keep written records. Most of the information we have about them comes from Roman writers. We know about Boudicca's rebellion from two Roman **historians**, called Tacitus and Dio Cassius. We have to be careful, though, when reading their books, because the Romans were enemies of the Celts. Their writings can be very unfair to Boudicca and her supporters.

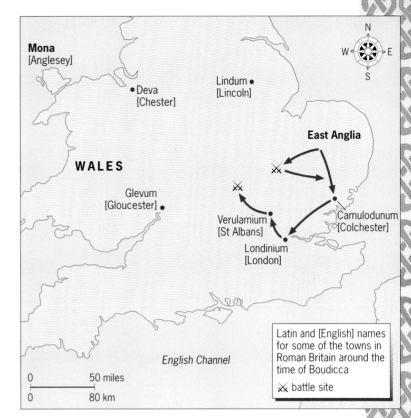

▲ This map shows southern Britain in AD 61, when Boudicca led her rebellion against the Romans. The blue arrows show Boudicca's route.

Key dates

55–54 BC	The Roman general Julius Caesar invades Celtic Britain, but fails to conquer it
About AD 30	Boudicca is born in East Anglia, in south-eastern England
AD 43	The Romans under the Emperor Claudius conquer Britain
About AD 48	Boudicca marries King Prasutagus of the Iceni and becomes Queen of the Iceni
AD 54–68	Rule of the Roman **Emperor** Nero
About AD 61	Boudicca leads a rebellion against Roman rule in south-eastern England
AD 61	Death of Queen Boudicca

Watch the dates

The letters 'BC' after a year date mean before the birth of Jesus Christ. The letters 'AD' stand for the Latin *anno domini* and mean that the date is after the birth of Christ.

Boudicca's early life

Although Boudicca is famous, very little is known about her early life. All we know is that she was born about the year AD 30 and that her family were probably important **aristocrats** who lived in the region now known as East Anglia. Boudicca is sometimes known by her Roman name of Boadicea, and she was probably named after the **Celtic** goddess of Victory, Boudiga.

Leaving home

Like the children of most Celtic families, Boudicca would have been sent away as a young girl to join the **household** of another aristocratic family. There she would have received her education, learning about the history and **customs** of her **tribe**. This exchange of children was an important way of building friendships and loyalty between different families and tribes.

While she was growing up, Boudicca was probably also trained to be a **warrior**. There were special training schools where girls as well as boys were taught how to fight with swords and spears, to ride horses and to drive **chariots**.

◀ The Celts were brilliant artists and their beautiful metalwork was famous throughout Europe. This **bronze** cow's head was probably the handle of a ceremonial bucket.

Celtic villages

The Celts lived in small villages in the countryside. They were a farming people, and most families owned a number of sheep, cattle and other animals. As Boudicca was born into a rich family, they would have owned many animals. They would probably have had a large **roundhouse** where they lived, ate and slept. They probably also had several other smaller thatched buildings which were used for keeping animals and storing food.

▲ This copy of a Celtic roundhouse has been built at Little Butser in Hampshire. The walls and roof were made of small tree trunks. The walls were filled in with wattle and daub (mud and sticks), and the roof was thatched with grasses.

The Celts

For 800 years, the Celts were the most powerful people in Europe. From about 800 BC, their **civilization** spread over most of mainland Europe and the British Isles. The Celtic tribes never united to form a single nation, and different languages were always spoken from tribe to tribe. The Celts were warlike people.

Queen Boudicca

Boudicca was expected to marry into another aristocratic family, or even into a royal family. The lands of the Iceni (you say 'eye-seen-eye') **tribe** were in the area known today as East Anglia. They lay to the south of her own tribal lands. Boudicca's family probably knew the royal family of the Iceni.

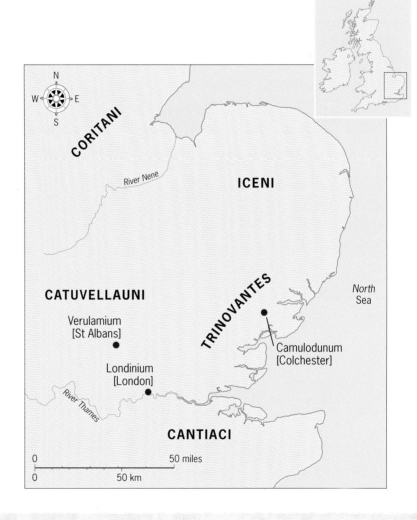

▶ The Iceni tribe occupied lands in the area of the present-day counties of Suffolk and Norfolk.

The Iceni

Like the other Celtic tribes, the Iceni were farmers. Their farmlands were well-known for being very **fertile**. This made them very rich. They also owned many horses, another form of great wealth at that time. When Boudicca married him, King Prasutagus was one of the richest of all the Celtic rulers in Britain.

A royal marriage

By about AD 48, when she would have been about eighteen years old, Boudicca had married Prasutagus, king of the Iceni. He was probably about ten years older than she was.

Their wedding would have been celebrated with offerings to the **Celtic** gods, followed by a magnificent feast. It would have been a splendid occasion, with guests invited from far away and delicious food and drink served for a whole day and night. The wedding celebrations would have been used as a display of wealth and power by the families of Boudicca and Prasutagus, and also as a way of making strong bonds between their two tribes.

Two daughters

Following her marriage, Boudicca became queen of the Iceni and went to live in her husband's royal **household**. After about a year, she gave birth to a daughter, followed a year later by another daughter. We do not know the names of the two princesses. Servants and nursemaids would have helped Boudicca raise the two girls, but it was the duty of every Celtic mother to make sure that her children received the correct education and training for adulthood.

▼ Celtic women spent much of their time looking after their families, preparing food, spinning wool and making clothes. You can see a loom for weaving cloth, a cooking fire and a stone for grinding corn inside this copy of a Celtic **roundhouse**.

The royal inheritance

King Prasutagus had been ruler of the Iceni for at least five years when he married Boudicca. **Celtic** kings did not always **inherit** their position from their fathers. They were often **elected** by the other noble men in the **tribe**, or became king by marrying the queen.

An unsuccessful rebellion

In about AD 49 or 50, a number of tribes in south-eastern England rose up against the Roman armies that had invaded England in AD 43. The **rebellion** was quickly crushed by the Romans. King Prasutagus had been one of the leaders of the rebellion, but he was allowed to keep his lands and his throne. However, the Romans now recognized him as a **client-king**, only accepted for as long as he did as he was told by them.

The death of Prasutagus

In about AD 61, King Prasutagus died. Boudicca was now about thirty years old and her two daughters were about eleven and twelve. Boudicca became **regent** of the Iceni, that is she became their ruler until a new king could be chosen by the tribal chiefs.

◄ This Roman coin shows the head of Nero, who was emperor at the time of Boudicca's rebellion. It was made in AD 55. The head behind Nero is his mother, Agrippina.

The king's will

Prasutagus had left a **will** when he died. This gave half his property and lands to the Roman **emperor**. As a client-king, who was under the control of the Romans, this was expected. He left the other half of his property to Boudicca and their two daughters. Prasutagus probably believed that he had left a peaceful settlement behind him, satisfying both the Romans and his family. Events were quickly to prove how wrong he was.

▶ Claudius was emperor at the time of the Roman invasion of Britain. This **bronze** head of Claudius was found in the River Alde in Suffolk.

The Roman conquest of Britain

In AD 43 the Roman emperor Claudius launched an invasion of Britain. Many of the British tribes, especially in southern England, surrendered to the invading army. Others continued to fight the Romans fiercely. It was to be many years before all the southern tribes were defeated. The Romans never succeeded in conquering Scotland.

The queen's fury

A few days after the death of King Prasutagus, the chief Roman **financial administrator** of Britain, who was called Catus Decianus, sent his officials to Boudicca's royal residence. They brought a message: as well as taking the property left to the Roman **emperor** by Prasutagus, Decianus was now also seizing the property that the king had left to Boudicca and her daughters.

Boudicca is forced out

Decianus ignored Prasutagus's **will** and proceeded to force Boudicca and her daughters off their land. He warned the chiefs of the Iceni **tribe** that their property would also be taken in the name of the Roman emperor.

The Roman **historian** Tacitus wrote: 'Kingdom and **household** alike were plundered [robbed] like prizes of war ... The Chieftains of the Iceni were deprived of their family estates as if the whole country had been handed over to the Romans. The king's own relatives were treated as **slaves**.'

▶ This 18th-century engraving shows Queen Boudicca speaking to her **warriors**. Many of them would have been from the Iceni tribe.

A public beating

Boudicca was outraged, and tried to prevent the Romans stealing her property. They decided to make an example of her in order to frighten the rest of her people. She was arrested by a group of soldiers and led to an open space.

There she was stripped naked and, in front of the Roman officials and her own horrified people, she was publicly beaten. Worse still, her two daughters were also badly treated by the Roman soldiers. This terrible behaviour was to show the Iceni that they were now totally under the control of the Romans.

▶ This small statue is of Epona, Celtic goddess of horses and fertility. Women often held positions of great power in the Celtic world and Epona was one of the most important of all the Celtic gods.

Celtic women

Celtic women enjoyed many privileges which were unheard of in other societies at that time. They could inherit property from their fathers and husbands. Roman law did not accept this, and this was one of the reasons why the Romans did not respect Prasutagus's will. Some Celtic women became very rich and a few even became rulers in their own right.

Boudicca attacks

Boudicca exploded with fury. The Romans had gone too far. She would make them pay dearly for their terrible action. The Iceni rallied round their queen, calling for **revenge** against the Romans. Many other **Celtic tribes** also supported her, united in their hatred of the Roman invaders.

Boudicca picks her target

Just beyond the southern borders of the Iceni lands lay the Roman town of Camulodunum, present-day Colchester in Essex. It served as the capital of the Roman government in Britain.

But Boudicca had another, far more important, reason for wanting to destroy Camulodunum. It was the headquarters of the soldiers who had committed the crime against herself and her daughters. Meanwhile, unaware that Boudicca was raising an army of **rebellion**, the Roman **governor** of Britain, Suetonius Paulinus, was far away attacking the island of Mona (Anglesey) in northern Wales.

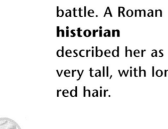

▶ This 19th-century illustration shows Boudicca leading her warriors into battle. A Roman **historian** described her as very tall, with long, red hair.

▲ Early Roman towns had buildings made of wood, which was why Camulodunum (Colchester) burned so quickly. Later buildings, such as this model of the temple at Camulodunum, were made of stone.

The attack on Camulodunum

Led by their **warrior** queen, her huge army poured out of the thick forests where they had been hiding. They reached Camulodunum and the army burst into the town.

The **garrison** and some of the people shut themselves into the temple. They managed to hold out for two days, but no help came. Boudicca's army overran the temple. All the inhabitants of Camulodunum – men, women and children – were killed. The town was set alight. It burned furiously. By the next day, it had been reduced to a blackened ruin. Boudicca now turned her attention to Londinium (London).

Roman towns

When the Romans conquered Britain, they quickly set about building new towns. These were usually built in the middle of Celtic tribal lands. They were important military centres for the Romans. The first of these new towns was at Camulodunum (Colchester). This was followed by others such as Glevum (Gloucester) and Lindum (Lincoln).

The rebellion sweeps on

Boudicca and her **warriors** had now tasted victory. Nothing was going to stop them as they swept south towards the town of Londinium.

A successful ambush

The Romans were in panic. Desperate messages were sent out all over Britain to try to raise **reinforcements**. Five thousand Roman soldiers were sent from a camp 129 km to the north of Camulodunum, but as they marched south they were **ambushed** and at least half of them were killed.

Decianus flees

Catus Decianus, whose terrible treatment of Boudicca and her family had led to the **rebellion**, was waiting for the extra soldiers to come to his rescue in Londinium. They never arrived. As news reached him that Boudicca and her army were getting closer and closer, he decided that he would have to abandon the town. He took all his staff with him and fled, leaving the people of Londinium to defend themselves.

▼ This modern painting by Richard Sorrel shows Londinium (London) on fire after Boudicca's attack. The city contained about 30,000 people, most of them merchants and their families.

Londinium falls

Meanwhile the Roman **governor**, Suetonius Paulinus, had marched his soldiers all the way from Wales and managed to reach Londinium before Boudicca. He decided, though, that he could not defend the town. It had no strong walls and his soldiers were exhausted after their rapid march from Wales. Tacitus wrote that Suetonius 'decided to save the whole situation by the sacrifice of a single city'.

Soon after Suetonius had left, Boudicca and her army swooped onto the town and killed everyone they found there. Once again, the buildings were set alight and burned to the ground.

▲ These skulls from the Roman period were found in the Walbrook River in London. They may have been victims of Boudicca's attack on Londinium.

Londinium – a merchant town

Londinium was not a military town like Camulodunum. It was a **merchant** town and Tacitus describes it as 'an important centre for businessmen and merchandise'. Londinium was built on the banks of the River Thames and trading ships brought goods from all over the **Roman Empire** to its harbour.

The fall of Verulamium

Leaving the smouldering ruins of Londinium behind them, Boudicca and her army turned north and headed for another Roman town. This was Verulamium, the present-day city of St Albans in Hertfordshire.

▲ There are many remains of Roman buildings at St Albans. Among them is this amphitheatre, which could hold 1600 spectators.

Verulamium must be sacrificed

Verulamium did not contain soldiers like Camulodunum, or Roman **merchants** like Londinium. It was inhabited only by British people, most of them from the Catuvellauni **tribe**. They supported the occupying Romans, so they were hated and despised by Boudicca and her followers.

The Roman **governor**, Suetonius, had by now retreated north with his soldiers to the Midlands region of England. He had decided that Verulamium would also have to be sacrificed before he was ready to fight Boudicca.

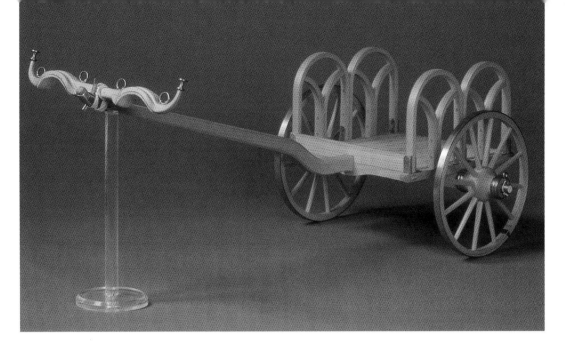

▲ This is a model of a Celtic war **chariot**. Chariots like this were made of wood, and held two people. A driver made the horses gallop at great speed. A warrior stood behind the driver to fight.

The citizens flee

As news of Boudicca's approaching army reached the town, many people packed up their belongings and took to the roads leading away from the town. There was now nowhere else for them to hide except in the forests and valleys of the surrounding countryside. Many more of the Catuvellauni people – perhaps as many as 15,000 of the old, the very young and the sick – had to be left behind. There was nothing they could do but wait for the end.

Like hungry wolves, Boudicca and her **warriors** pounced on Verulamium and tore it apart. Everyone left behind was killed. Once more the buildings were burned to the ground. Boudicca had now destroyed three important Roman towns. It seemed that nothing could stop her.

Roman roads

The Romans constructed a network of roads across Britain, which enabled their soldiers to march quickly from one place to another. The roads were long and straight, and paved with stone slabs. **Drainage channels** on either side allowed rainwater to run off. Trees were cleared away from near roads to make it difficult for enemy soldiers to hide and **ambush** the Romans.

Boudicca misses her chance

Boudicca and her army may have looked **invincible** when they left the ruined town of Verulamium, but events were now running out of control and there was little Boudicca could do to stop them.

A vital mistake

It was now that Boudicca made a great mistake. As she and her **warriors** were rampaging across the countryside, Suetonius was keeping out of her way. He was in a very weak position, so it was at this point that Boudicca should have attacked his army. She missed this chance of victory, though. This gave the Romans precious extra time to regroup and prepare for the final battle.

An unpaid army

While Boudicca's followers were strong in numbers and enthusiastic, in most other ways they did not match up to the efficient and well-trained Roman army. Her army was not being paid, as the Roman soldiers were. While Boudicca's warriors were away from their homes, their farms were being neglected. Crops had not been sown in the fields. There would be no harvest and they would soon run out of food supplies. If that happened, the warriors would start to return to their farms and the **rebellion** would collapse.

▶ A Celtic sword had a long iron blade which was razor sharp along both edges. This one has a handle in the shape of a human figure.

Suetonius makes his move

It was Suetonius who now decided that he must finally confront Boudicca's army. Tacitus tells us: 'By now Suetonius Paulinus had with him the XIV **Legion** and a detachment of the XX, together with auxiliary (supporting) troops from the nearest fort, about 10,000 men, and he decided to make an end of delay and join battle.'

◀ This bronze statue from about 150 BC shows a typical Roman **legionary** soldier.

Celtic weapons

A **Celtic** warrior's favourite weapon was the sword. This was used to slash at the enemy soldiers rather than stab them. A Celtic army would usually start fighting by throwing spears at the enemy, or sending small, deadly stones whizzing from leather **sling-shots**. The warriors then charged in with their swords, using daggers for stabbing at close quarters.

The final battle

At last Boudicca received news about where Suetonius and his soldiers were hiding. It may be that Suetonius had decided to let her **scouts** find out where he was, so that he could lead Boudicca and her army into a trap.

Historians today are still uncertain where exactly the final battle between Boudicca and the Romans took place, but it was probably somewhere in the region of the counties of Warwickshire and Leicestershire in the West Midlands.

The battle site

Suetonius chose his site for the battle very carefully. Tacitus wrote that the **governor** and his army were in a narrow valley with a wood behind them. They positioned themselves at the top of a steep slope at the end of the valley, giving them a much better position than the British below them.

▶ This tombstone from Gloucester shows a **Thracian** cavalryman riding down a British warrior.

Boudicca rouses her warriors

Tacitus tells that before the battle began, Boudicca gave one last, rousing speech to her followers. She drove in her **chariot** amongst her **warriors** with her two young daughters in front of her. She reminded her followers of the conquest and robbery of their lands by the hated Romans and warned them that if they did not win this battle all would be lost for ever.

Then she said, 'You will win this battle, or die. That is what I, a woman, plan to do! Let the men live in **slavery** if they will.' At the end of this speech, the Britons let out a great shout and called on their gods to support them.

▲ These three gold torques were made in the first century BC, and were found in Norfolk. Celtic warriors believed that wearing a torque round their necks gave them magical protection.

Battledress

Celtic warriors protected themselves in battle with long shields made of wood and leather. They usually wore thick woollen shirts over baggy trousers with close-fitting helmets of leather, iron or bronze on their heads. However, they often went into battle wearing nothing at all except a thick metal band called a **torque** round their necks.

The tide is stopped

B ritish **warriors** started to pour into the narrow valley, shouting and singing as they came. The Roman **historians** tell us that as many as 100,000 British faced a Roman army of no more than 13,000.

The Roman formation

The Romans were drawn up in a straight line at the top end of the valley. Suetonius had positioned his **legionaries** in the centre of the line with more soldiers on either side of them. At both ends of the line were the cavalry, on horseback.

Attack!

Boudicca and Suetonius then gave their armies the order to attack. The British charged forward, blowing horns and shouting their war cries. The Roman soldiers sent out a shower of spears and many of the British were killed instantly. The Roman cavalry then moved in from the sides and prevented the British from spreading out.

The Romans were far better trained and disciplined than the British. When one row of soldiers had attacked, it moved back. The next row would come forward in wave after wave.

▲ The carving on this stone coffin shows a battle between the Romans and the Gauls, who were Celts from northern France.

The British are defeated

There were now far too many British warriors crowded into the valley. They were packed in so tightly that they could not use their long swords against the Romans. Thousands of Boudicca's warriors were killed. According to Tacitus, 'there fell 80,000 of the Britons, with a loss to our soldiers of about 400'.

Boudicca's army had at last been defeated and the British **uprising** against the Romans had been crushed.

▲ The Romans wrote how tall and impressive the Celtic warriors looked, with magnificent bodies and terrifying battle cries. Some painted their bodies and combed lime through their hair to make it stand on end. This is a modern-day renactment.

Battle plans

Boudicca's army were in a weaker position. The Romans were highly trained and followed a strict battle plan. The **Celts'** only plan was to surprise their enemy. If this did not succeed, they sent in warriors on horseback and in **chariots** to mow the enemy down, followed by the rest of the army. In this final battle, Boudicca was unable to use any of these moves.

The death of Boudicca

Boudicca herself probably led her **warriors** into battle against the Romans. She charged at the head of her army in her **chariot**, her red hair flowing over her shoulders and her two daughters by her side.

Poison

It is believed that Boudicca did not die on the battlefield. She managed to escape with her daughters to a hiding place. There, it is said, she gave the two princesses poison to drink and then drank some herself.

Boudicca knew that if they were captured alive a terrible end would be in store for them. They would be taken in chains to Rome and forced to walk through the streets in a victory parade. Then they would be killed. Instead, we think Queen Boudicca and her daughters died quietly and bravely on the land they had fought so hard to defend from the Roman invaders.

▶ This Victorian marble statue shows Boudicca and her two daughters after their final battle with the Romans. No one really knows how they died or where they were buried.

Where is Boudicca buried?

What happened to Boudicca and her daughters after they died is not certain. Dio Cassius writes only that she was given a 'costly burial', fit for such a great queen.

Much later, in the 17th century, a story grew up that Boudicca was buried at the ancient site of Stonehenge, but this is not likely. Other suggested sites for her grave include one in her own family lands in Norfolk, another in Hampstead in north London and even one under Platform 8 of King's Cross Station in London!

We will never really know what became of Boudicca's body. Like the beginning of her life, very little is known about her end.

▼ Rich Celts, like Boudicca, were often buried with their chariots and even their horses. This Celtic chariot was found in a burial at Garton-on-the-Wolds in Yorkshire.

Celtic burials

The **Celts** believed that when a person died they went on a journey to another world. They were buried with all the things that would make their journey and their life in the next world as comfortable as possible. Jewellery, clothes and plates of food were often placed in the grave.

After Boudicca

After the final battle, the Romans hunted down the survivors from Boudicca's army and killed them. Suetonius was determined to punish those who had rebelled against him. He was ruthless in his **revenge**.

Punishing the Iceni

Suetonius singled out the Iceni for particular punishment. The Iceni managed to keep up their fight against the Romans on and off over the next year, but eventually they were all either killed, or captured and made into **slaves**. Their farms were destroyed and their possessions stolen.

Then Suetonius was recalled to Rome. He was replaced by a new **governor** of Britain, called Petronius Turpilianus, who decided that the Britons had been punished enough for the **rebellion**. From then on, the **Celtic** people were treated more respectfully by their Roman rulers.

▲ Remains of a Roman fort in Northumberland. After Boudicca's rebellion was crushed, the Romans built forts all over Britain to prevent any more uprisings. Britain remained part of the Roman Empire for nearly 400 years.

The Celts become Roman Britons

The Romans continued to rule Britain for nearly 400 years. As the years went by, the Celts gradually changed to the Roman way of life. They took up the **customs** and religion of the Romans and eventually forgot their own. They married Romans and with each passing generation they gradually changed from being Celtic Britons into Roman Britons.

Boudicca's reputation

Although Boudicca's rebellion failed, her name is still one of the most famous in British history. She is recognized as a woman of great courage, who rallied her people in one last, desperate attempt to free her lands from control by foreign armies. She dared to challenge the mighty **Roman Empire**. Boudicca is remembered as the **warrior** queen who chose to die, rather than accept defeat and become a **slave**.

▶ This Celtic bronze shield is decorated with red glass. It was found in the River Thames at Battersea, London.

Glossary

ambush   surprise attack by soldiers who have been waiting in hiding

aristocrat   member of the noble or upper class

bronze   metal made by mixing copper and tin

Celts   the people of Britain and much of Europe at the time Boudicca lived

chariot   two-wheeled vehicle pulled by horses

civilization   human society and how it is organized

client-king   king who owed his authority to another ruler, such as the Roman emperor

customs   long-established traditions of a tribe or people

drainage channel   channel built along a roadside to allow water to drain away

elect   choose someone to hold a position by voting for them

emperor   ruler who reigns over a large area of land, called an empire

fertile   rich soil that produces good crops

financial administrator   person who controls and looks after money

garrison   group of soldiers who defend a town or fort

governor   Roman official who ruled a province (region) of the Roman Empire

historian   person who studies or writes about history

household   people living in a house, including the family and any servants

independence   being independent, or free from outside control

inherit   receive something, such as property or a title when someone dies

invincible   unbeatable

legion   Roman army group, consisting of three to five thousand men

legionaries   soldiers of a legion

merchant   person who buys and sells goods

rebellion   organized opposition to a government or some other authority

regent   person who rules on behalf of someone else

reinforcements   extra soldiers who give added strength and support to an army

revenge   act of retaliating for a wrong or injury received

Roman Empire   lands ruled by the Romans. In Boudicca's time the Roman Empire covered most of Europe and northern Africa.

roundhouse   a circular Celtic house

scout   person sent out to gain information

slave   servant who was the property of his or her master. A slave had no personal freedom.

sling-shot   weapon made of a loop of leather in which a stone is whirled around and then let fly

Thracian   someone from around the area that is now Turkey

torque   thick necklace made of twisted metal, worn by Celtic warriors

tribe   group of people with a common descent, land and culture

uprising   fighting in a rebellion

warrior   fighters in battles

will   a legal document in which a person says how their property and money should be divided up after their death

Timeline

Further reading & websites

Boadicea: Warrior Queen of the Celts, John Mathews, Firebird Books 1988

Explore History Series: Romans, Anglo Saxons & Vikings in Britain, Haydn Middleton, Heinemann Library, 2001

Famous People, Famous Lives: Boudicca, Franklin Watts

On the Trail of The Celts in Britain, Peter Chrisp, Watts, 1999

Step into the Celtic World, Fiona Macdonald, Heinemann, 2000

Heinemann Explore – an online resource from Heinemann. For Key Stage 2 history go to *www.heinemannexplore.com*

www.thehistorychannel.com

Places to visit

Colchester, Essex

Museum of London, London

Norwich Castle, Norfolk

St Albans, Hertfordshire

Index

Titles in the Life and World of series include:

Hardback   0 431 14765 5

Hardback   0 431 14771 X

Hardback   0 431 14774 4

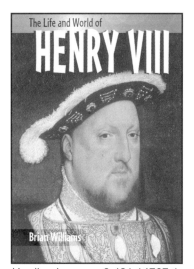

Hardback   0 431 14767 1

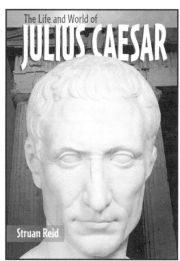

Hardback   0 431 14775 2

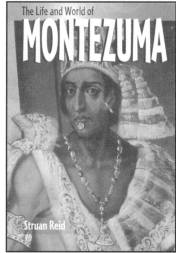

Hardback   0 431 14763 9

Hardback   0 431 14769 8

Hardback   0 431 14761 2

Find out about the other titles in this series on our website www.heinemann.co.uk/library